Abingdon's
Christmas Drama
COLLECTION

4 SHORT DRAMAS

 Abingdon Press

ABINGDON'S CHRISTMAS DRAMA COLLECTION

Copyright © 1995 by Abingdon Press
All rights reserved.

ISBN 0-687-005752

95 96 97 98 00 01 02 03 04 05 - 10 9 8 7 6 5 4 2 1

MANUFACTURED IN THE UNITED STATES OF AMERICA

CONTENTS

PLAYS

POEMS AND RECITATIONS

EMMANUEL—GOD WITH US

A Dramatic Worship Service for Christmas

by Georgianna Summers

Introduction

This service can be adapted in a variety of ways for large or small congregations. It calls for two readers (Readers 1 and 2) at the front of the sanctuary at pulpit and lectern, and four other readers either at the back or at various places in the congregation. Reader 5 (the voice of Jesus) should read from the back or through the speaker system and not be seen by the congregation. Reader 1 can be the minister.

The music can be done entirely by the congregation, or appropriate choir anthems or solos can be substituted for some of the carols. The service can also be dramatized with adults, youth, and/or children portraying the parts of Mary, Joseph, shepherds, etc. in tableaux.

The use of four Advent candles and a Christ candle can also be an effective way to dramatize the birth of Jesus. If the service is used for Christmas Eve, a candlelighting ceremony for the entire congregation can follow. If this is done, as people arrive ushers should give each person over eight years of age a small candle with a cardboard drip catcher to be used at the end of the service. Give the instructions about spreading the light before the service begins so that the continuity is not broken.

EMMANUEL—GOD WITH US

READER 1: Thus says God, the Lord,
Who created the heavens and stretched them out,
Who spread forth the earth and what comes from it,
Who gives breath to the people upon it
And spirit to those who walk in it:
"I am the Lord, I have called you in
        righteousness,
I have taken you by the hand and kept you;
I have given you as a covenant to the people,
A light to the nations,
To open the eyes that are blind,

To bring out from the prison those who sit in
        darkness,
Arise, shine: for your light has come,
And the glory of the Lord has risen upon you."
                                —Isaiah 42:5-7; 60:1 (RSV)

Carol: *"Angels from the Realms of Glory"*

READER 2:   Matthew 1:18-23

Carol: *"O Come, O Come Emmanuel"*

(During the singing of this carol, the four Advent candles may be lit.)

READER 1:   Emmanuel—God with us—and truly he was—
        Walking among his people,
        Preaching good news to the poor,
        Healing the sick, opening the eyes of the blind,
        Feeding the hungry,
        Freeing those in bondage to their lesser selves.
        He came to his own people, and they knew
                him not,
        And still he comes—
        But do *we* know him?

READER 2:   Luke 2:1-7

(During the reading of this scripture the Advent candles should be extinguished and the Christ candle lit. Also, if the scene is dramatized, Mary and Joseph should enter here.)

Carol: *"Away in a Manger"* or *"Silent Night"*

(If a choir or soloist is used, an appropriate selection might be "Sweet Little Jesus Boy")

READER 3:   How was I, the innkeeper, to know him?
        His parents looked like ordinary people,
        Tired and dirty from traveling.
        I did the best I could for them.

6

Of course, if I had known who he was,
I might have given them my room,
But you have to think of yourself too,
And you can't help every needy person
Who knocks on your door.

READER 2: Luke 2:8-14

Carol: *"It Came Upon the Midnight Clear"*

READER 4: We had a vision, we shepherds,
And when it was over we said,
"Let's go over to Bethlehem and see for
    ourselves."
And we went quickly and found Mary and Joseph
And the babe lying in a manger.
But we wondered as did those we told—
Awed by our experience,
And not quite sure how he would bring us peace
    and save us—
From the Romans perhaps?
We didn't know what kind of saving he would
    bring.

READER 2: Matthew 2:1-11

Carol: *"What Child Is This?"*

(If desired, an offering can be taken at this time.)

READER 1: And did *they* know him, the wise men?
They looked for him in Herod's palace
Perhaps they thought that's where a king should
    be born.
But did they know then that his kingdom was not
    of this world—
The kingdom of God within us—
And that he comes to us in each person we meet,
Regardless of their station in life?

7

READER 2:   Luke 2:21-24; 39-40

READER 1:   And when he was about thirty years of age, he came to the Jordan River and was baptized by John. Then he was led by the Spirit for forty days in the wilderness, tempted by the devil.

READER 2:   Luke 4:14-17

READER 5:   *(Voice of Jesus)*
The Spirit of the Lord is upon me,
Because he has anointed me to preach good news
        to the poor.
He has sent me to proclaim release to the captives
And recovering of sight to the blind,
To set at liberty those who are oppressed,
To proclaim the acceptable year of the Lord.
(Pause)
Today this scripture has been fulfilled in your hearing.

READER 6:   We didn't think he was anyone special,
We villagers who had seen him grow up among us.
We knew his father—Joseph, the carpenter;
His mother, Mary; his brothers and sisters.
"Where did he get all this wisdom?" we asked,
"And how does he get off thinking
God has anointed him for something special?"
We asked for healing miracles,
But he couldn't do much for us in Nazareth
Because we didn't recognize who he was.

Hymn: *"We Would See Jesus"*

READER 1:   And still he comes to preach good news to *us,*
        the poor—
Some in things and all in soul.
To bring release to *us,* the captives,
Imprisoned by our fears and anxieties.

8

To open our eyes—blinded by prejudice,
entrenched ideas, hatred of self and others.

READER 5:   *(Voice of Jesus)*
Seek first the kingdom of God. *(Pause)*
Fear not, oh you of little faith. *(Pause)*
You are of value. Even the hairs of your head are
        numbered. *(Pause)*
Love your neighbor as yourself. *(Pause)*
Forgive others the wrongs they have done to you.

READER 2:   And so he was the word made flesh—
Emmanuel—God with us—
In him was life,
And the life was the light of humankind.

READER 1:   Where shall we find him then,
Walking among us?

READER 3:   In soup kitchens—feeding the hungry.

READER 4:   By sick beds—ministering to the suffering.

READER 6:   At bargaining tables—negotiating for peace.

READER 2::   In protest marches—calling for justice.

READER 1:   And how shall we know him?

READER 3:   By the eyes of the lonely, longing for friendship.

READER 4:   In the faces of the homeless, searching for shelter.

READER 6:   By the wounds of the abused, pleading for healing.

READER 2:   In the cries of the oppressed, calling for freedom.

READER 5:   Inasmuch as you do it unto one of the least of
these, you do it unto me.

(If the service is used for a Christmas Eve candlighting service, extinguish the lights at this point leaving only the Christ candle lit. Have candlighters come forward to take the light from the Christ candle and light the candles of each person seated at the ends of the pews. They in turn will light the candles of the persons next to them, and so on down each pew. While this is being done, Readers 1 and 2 will read the following Scripture, pausing between each reading. When the Scripture is finished and enough light has been spread for people to see, start singing "O Little Town of Bethlehem.")

READER 1:   The light will shine in the darkness,
And the darkness has never put it out.
Take the light now from the Christ candle;
Spread it among you from person to person.

READER 2:   This is the message we have heard from him and proclaim to you, that God is light and in God is no darkness at all. If we walk in the light, as God is in the light, we have fellowship with one another, and the blood of Jesus, God's son, cleanses us from all sin. For the darkness is passing away, and the real light is already shining.
(Pause)

READER 1:   Dear friends, let us love one another, because love comes from God. Whoever loves is a child of God and knows God. Whoever does not love does not know God, for God is love. And God showed love for us by sending Jesus into the world so that we might have life through him.
(Pause)

READER 2:   This is what love is: it is not that we have loved God, but that God loved us and sent his son to be the means by which our sins are forgiven. Dear friends, if this is how God loved us, then we should love one another.
(Pause)

10

READER 1: You are the light of the world. A city set on a hill cannot be hid. Nor do we light a lamp and put it under a bushel, but on a stand, and it gives light to all in the house. Let your light so shine that others may see your good works and give glory to God who is in heaven.

Carol: *"O Little Town of Bethlehem"*

BENEDICTION *(by the pastor)*

Take the light of Christ now out into the world.
Feed the hungry.
Give drink to those who thirst.
Welcome the stranger.
Clothe the naked.
Visit the sick and those in prison, remembering
Inasmuch as you do it unto one of the least of these, you do it unto him. Amen.

CHRISTMAS IN THE TOY SHOP
by Louise Gouge

This short play can be presented in a church using children as the actors or in a mall with more mature actors. In the mall, the skit serves as a witnessing tool and an opening to invite shoppers to a church Christmas program.

This scene is a toy shop in a mall with a rustic roof jutting out over the entrance. Toys and dolls are displayed on tables across the back and sides of the store. A sign announces "Toys: new and used."

Characters

Speaking parts:

TOYMAKER *(a "little old" man or woman)*

TIFFANY, **beauty queen** doll

DESERT DAN **soldier** action figure

KING MIDAS **wrestler** action figure
(wears shorts, gold wrestling belt and cape)

GAME PLAYER
(computer game, rectangular shape with screen in center, etc.)

RAG DOLL BOY

RAG DOLL GIRL

Non-speaking parts:

BASKETBALL PLAYER with ball

BICYCLE OR MOTOR SCOOTER *(a person dressed creatively)*

STUFFED TOYS

BABY DOLL *(an actual toy, lines to be spoken by someone nearby)*

13

CHRISTMAS IN THE TOY SHOP

TOYMAKER: *(Enters, bustles about arranging toys and humming a Christmas song.)*
Oh, how I love Christmas! The season is so full of wonder and joy. *(Adjusting a toy)*
Ah, yes, everything is just perfect. Tomorrow people will come and choose one of you for their dear children. *(He looks fondly at the two rag dolls).* There, there, don't look so sad, my little ones. Surely this year someone will choose you. See, you're all washed and mended, good as new. Well, almost good as new. Hmm. Maybe I've better mark your price down a little more.
(Changes price with magic marker.)
There, that should do it. Sleep well, my little ones. Once you belong to a child, things will get very busy for you. Goodnight, little friends. Goodnight.

(Exits humming Christmas song. As he leaves, the toys watch with eyes only. Once he is out of sight, they begin to move. Each toy takes on an identity. Basketball player, bicycle and stuffed toys react to lines of speaking toys.)

TIFFANY: *(Yawning and stretching)*
Oh, my. I'm so beautiful.
(Gets off table and moves to center stage.)
I can't wait until tomorrow. Every little girl wants a Tiffany doll. I'll bet I'm the first toy to be chosen.
(She inspects her finger nails and fluffs her hair)

DESERT DAN: *(Comes center stage)*
No way! Desert Dan is the toy of choice this year. Even girls want to play soldier these days.

KING MIDAS: *(Joins them center stage.)*
Listen to ME, all you toys. Nobody but nobody beats out King Midas. Every thing I touch turns to gold.

(He holds up his gold championship wrestling belt.)
All the kids want wrestler action figures like ME!
I'm gonna tromp all you guys at the cash register.
You won't even know what hit you. I'm gonna . . .
(Game Player comes center stage, screen blinking)
Whoa! Who do you think you are?

GAME PLAYER: You're all so boring. Kids love computer games better than anything. No one ever gets tired of *me!*

BABY DOLL: Mama! Mama!

DESERT DAN: Only babies like silly toys like you. Kids like action toys . . . like ME!

(Rag dolls are huddled together, listening to the conversation and looking very sad)

TIFFANY: *(Notices rag dolls)*
Oh, my goodness. Someone forgot to throw out the trash. Whoops! Oh my, you poor little things. You're all . . . uh, RAGS!

KING MIDAS: Hey, what do you think you're doing here? This is a TOY store.

RAG BOY: We ARE toys. Really, we are.

RAG GIRL: Really we are.

TIFFANY: But you're . . . well . . . you're HOMEMADE! What are you doing here? No one will ever buy you, especially when they see ME.

KING MIDAS: You got no pizzazz, man. No STYLE! Take a look at ME. *(Ha flaunts his cape and jewelry)*

GAME PLAYER: *(Strutting around)*
You can't challenge kids like *I* can. See my screen light up! My new games are all action!

DESERT DAN:	You can't even stand up!
RAG BOY:	Oh, yes we can!
RAG GIRL:	We can!

(The two rag dolls struggle to their feet and wobble around, then slump down on floor. The other dolls laugh at them.)

RAG BOY:	Well, sort of . . .
RAG GIRL:	*(Sniffling)* Sort of . . .
RAG BOY:	*(Comforts her)* Don't cry, please don't cry. Remember when we were loved?
RAG GIRL:	But it's been so long. I just want to be useful again, to bring a tiny smile to someone.
BABY DOLL:	Mama! Mama!
TIFFANY:	*(Yawns with boredom)* Well, I'd better get my beauty rest. I'll be busy, busy, busy all too soon.
DESERT DAN:	Get a life, lazy. I'm gonna practice maneuvers. *(He poses with his gun and pretends to shoot.)*
KING MIDAS:	Move over, pip-squeak. I'm the tough guy here.
GAME PLAYER:	Look at my latest action game! ZIP! BLAT! ZAPPO! I'm the STAR of Christmas this year!
BABY DOLL:	Mama! Mama!

(Chaos reigns as all the toys boast and clamor. Basketball player bounces ball, stuffed toys argue with each other. Rag dolls comfort each other.)

TOYMAKER: *(Entering)* What's this? What's this?

(All toys freeze where they are)

Oh, don't try to fool me. I saw you. I HEARD you. Is this the way I made you . . . all selfish and rude?

(All toys look ashamed)

Did I forget to tell you that I made each of you especially for Christmas? Or did I forget to tell you what Christmas is all about? Ah, that's it! You don't understand. Well, my little ones, let me tell you a story . . .
Once, long ago, the world was full of selfishness and meanness . . . just like today. But God up in heaven decided to show us how to love one another. God didn't send a beautiful angel to show us . . .
(looks at TIFFANY, who blushes, ashamed of her boasting.)

God didn't send a soldier with weapons of war . . .

(DAN looks down, embarrassed, tries to hide his gun.)

And God didn't send a strong and mighty KING . . .

(MIDAS shrugs with guilt.)

Instead, God chose a humble couple to take care of His special gift to all the world . . .

(places RAG BOY and RAG GIRL on either side of GAME PLAYER)

God's very own Son, born in a stable and placed in a manger.
(He looks at GAME PLAYER.)

Hmmmm. What can we use for a manger?

(GAME PLAYER looks around, smiles sheepishly, shrugs, then folds himself up until his box becomes the manger.)

TOYMAKER: *(places BABY DOLL on top of GAME PLAYER'S box)*
God sent His angel to stand watch over that little stable . . .
(moves Tiffany upstage, she lights up with joy.)
He called shepherds from the hillside to come and see His Lamb . . .
(places a cloak on Dan and trades his gun for a shepherd's crook.)
And he called mighty kings to come from afar and worship the true KING . . .
(places MIDAS to the side to kneel down and makes his belt into gift of gold.)
So you see, my little ones, when we look beyond ourselves, we see the real meaning of Christmas. A baby who came to bring peace on earth, good will toward men.

(He places a star on the basketball, and basketball player holds it high above his head. Bicycle becomes a cow, stuffed animals are sheep, etc. Recorded CHRISTMAS MUSIC can play in the background. As the toys all freeze into a Nativity Scene, the pastor can give an invitation or workers in a mall can pass out tracts or invitations to a church service.)

NO ROOM

A Christmas Play
by Louise Gouge

This play can be presented in a church sanctuary. Center stage is an expensive living room with couch, chairs, coffee table, TV. There are Christmas decorations and a tree with lights. On stage left is the "front yard" where the nativity scene will appear. Choir should be seated in choir loft.

Characters

FATHER

MOTHER

WENDY, age 11

SARAH, age 14

JOHNNY, age 9

Cousin MARGARET

Neighborhood children:
JENNIFER, BRIAN, BILLY, LITTLE CHILD,
JIMMY, JOEY, SUSAN,
several others ages 5-8

SCENE 1

Family enters from stage right. Father carries briefcase, Mother carries mail, girls have schoolbooks, son has football.

FATHER: *(plops down in a chair)*
Man, what a day!

JOHNNY: Dad, will you play football with me?

WENDY: *(whining)* Oh, I missed "General Hospital."
(or other favorite soap opera)

FATHER:	Hey, honey, what's for dinner? I worked hard today. I'm starved!
JOHNNY:	Dad, can we play football until supper?
SARAH:	*(to Wendy)* "General Hospital" is stupid.
MOTHER:	*(reading mail) Dear,* I thought I told you to pay this department store bill before the first of the month. Now how am I going to charge the rest of our presents?
FATHER:	Don't bother me with that now. What's for dinner?
JOHNNY:	Dad, can we *please* play football?
WENDY:	"General Hospital" is better than dumb Tom Cruise movies. *(or current teen idol)*
JOHNNY:	Da-ad!
FATHER:	Quiet, Johnny. Woman, what's for dinner?
MOTHER:	*(reading a letter)* Oh, no! I can't believe it!
FATHER:	What's the matter now!
MOTHER:	It's a letter from my Cousin Margaret. She's coming for Christmas!
FATHER:	Margaret? You mean. . . the . . . the missionary? *(groans)*
MOTHER:	None other. She says, "I'm writing in time so that you can let me know if it's not convenient." When did she send this? *(looking at envelope)* Oh, good grief! She sent it two months ago. I guess the mail can't get through with the trouble they've had over there. That means she's coming tomorrow!

SARAH: Mom, who's Cousin Margaret?

MOTHER: *(looking at Father)* You'll find out soon enough.

Choir Interlude: *"Joy to the World"*

SCENE II

Same setting, next morning. Family is ready to leave for the day, books, briefcase, etc. in hand. Simple change of clothes or adding a sweater or jacket can suggest a new day.

FATHER: It's seven-thirty in the morning! What a ridiculous time for her plane to arrive! Well, I'll just tell you one thing. She'd better get here soon or she'll be sitting on the front steps until this evening.

SARAH: Mother, Wendy's been in my closet again!

WENDY: I have not.

JOHNNY: Dad, can you help me with my science project tonight?

FATHER: Get your mother to help you. I'm no good with science.

JOHNNY: But, Dad, you work for NASA. *(or local chemical company)*

MOTHER: Quiet, everyone. She's here. *(goes to stage right, opens "door," and lets in Cousin Margaret)* Margaret! Come in! How nice to see you! *(insincerely)*

MARGARET: Oh, I'm so glad to be here. What a lovely home you have. And a lovely family, too. Do you

children know that I pray for each one of you
every day? Your grandmother writes and tells me
all about you. And here I am, finally getting to
meet you.

(There is an awkward pause.)

MOTHER: Well, here you are. Isn't that nice?

MARGARET: Do you remember when you two got married
fifteen years ago? I sang at your wedding, then
left that same week for the mission field. Hasn't
the Lord been good to all of us? You have this
wonderful home and family, and I have been
blessed in my work of translating the New
Testament into the Lumi language. Do you
children know that over two thousand tribes and
ethnic groups around the world still do not have
God's Word in their own language?

*(The children look at each other and shrug. Father and Mother look
embarrassed.)*

FATHER: Uh, well, listen, Margaret . . . sorry, but we have to
leave. Work and school, you know.

MOTHER: Make yourself at home. We'll be back around six
o'clock tonight.

WENDY: Do you know what a television is?

JOHNNY: Are you my cousin or my aunt or what?

MOTHER: *(embarrassed, hurries the children out the door)*
Bye, now.

MARGARET: *(watches them leave, then turns her eyes upward in prayer)*
Oh, Lord, it's just as bad as Grandmother wrote.
My cousins are so busy with their jobs and making

money, they've forgotten you. And the children! They don't even seem to know who You are. It seems so strange. The poor people I've been with love You so much and are thankful for all Your care. But despite all these possessions You've given my cousins, they don't seem to want You to live here. I guess there's just no room.

Choir or Solo: *"No Room"* by Lanny Wolfe, or other appropriate song

SCENE III

Margaret, Sarah, and Wendy are seated in the living room making some sort of craft.

WENDY: Cousin Margaret, it's sure been nice having you with us this past week.

SARAH: Yeah, I never knew anything about the Philippines, but you make it so interesting.

WENDY: Well, Tom Cruise never made a movie there, so of course, you don't know anything about it.
(Sarah makes a face at her.)

MARGARET: It's a wonderful place. And the people are very open to hearing the Gospel.

SARAH: What's the big deal about translating the Bible? I mean, it's just an old book.

MARGARET: Oh, it's more than an old book. It's God's Book.

WENDY: Really?

SARAH:	But what's it all about? We have a big old Bible on the table there, but it looks too big and boring, like *Moby Dick* or *Gone with the Wind*. Could you just give us a shortened version of it?
MARGARET:	*(laughing)* I can't really give you a shortened version. That would leave out too many wonderful Bible stories. But I can tell you the main message of the Bible.
WENDY:	Cool! Another story!
SARAH:	Your stories are great!
MARGARET:	First of all, the Bible tells us that we are all sinners.
WENDY:	Not me! I'm no sinner. Sinners take drugs and stuff!
SARAH:	Hey, I even keep my room clean. I'm not a sinner . . . am I?
MARGARET:	Oh, yes, dear. We have all sinned and come short of the glory and goodness of God. That proves we are sinners. Haven't you ever stolen a cookie? Or told a lie? Even a little one? Have you ever been very, very angry with your sister?
	(Both girls look at each other, then down.)
	You see? We sin because we are sinners, and sinners will never be allowed to have eternal life in heaven with God.
WENDY:	Do you mean when we die we're going to . . .
SARAH:	*(breaking in)* . . . the other place?
MARGARET:	I'm afraid so. But now comes the good side of the story. God made a way so we don't have to be lost. God sent His son Jesus to earth . . .

SARAH:	Baby Jesus . . . that's what Christmas is about! *(She is proud of herself for knowing this.)*
MARGARET:	Yes, it did begin at Christmas. God sent His Son to earth as a gift for us. But Jesus grew up and became a man, then He died on a cross to . . .
WENDY:	Wait a minute. That's Easter. I know that much!
MARGARET:	The message of Jesus is not complete without telling the whole story. Christmas is a wonderful celebration of Jesus' birth. But it was His death and resurrection that gives us eternal life. When He died, He paid for our sins.
SARAH:	Then why did you say we have to go to "a-hem" *(she clears her throat)* if He paid for our sins?
MARGARET:	God gave us a free will. We have the choice to accept His free gift by believing in His Son. Some people don't. But if we believe, we become His children. We are saved.
SARAH:	I want to be a child of God.
WENDY:	Me, too. I want to accept God's free gift.
MARGARET:	That would make me so happy. And it will make God happy, too. Do you want to pray right now?
SARAH:	I do. Dear God, I want to be Your child. Please forgive me for my sins.
WENDY:	Dear Jesus, I accept Your free gift. I want to come to heaven and be with You. And God . . . I'm sorry for being mean to my big sister.

Choir, solo, or duet for Sarah and Wendy: *"We Are the Reason"* by David Meece or other appropriate song.

SCENE IV

Same scene. Margaret, Wendy, and Sarah are reading the Bible silently. Mother and Father enter stage right. The others do not hear their conversation until Sarah looks up.

FATHER: I have to admit having Margaret here has been a lot nicer than I expected.

MOTHER: She really gets along well with the children. And there just seems to be a peacefulness in the house with her here.

SARAH: *(noticing her parents)*
Mom! Dad! We have something to tell you.

WENDY: We've saved!

SARAH: We accepted God's free gift of Jesus and now we're His children.

WENDY: Mom, Dad, you have to accept God's gift, too! Did you know that Jesus died for your sins?

Mother and Father exchanged embarrassed looks.

FATHER: Honey, I've been a Christian since I was eight years old.

MOTHER: I was twelve when I accepted Jesus.

The girls look at each other in disbelief.

WENDY: Then how come you never told us about Him?

Father and Mother are speechless.

MARGARET: Oh, look out the window . . . carolers!

Small ensemble of carolers stand outside the "door" and sing: "The First Noel" As the carolers sing, the family listens.

MOTHER:	It's so good to hear the Christmas music. It reminds me of when I was a girl growing up in the church. Oh, honey, I can't believe how far we've let our faith slip!
FATHER:	I know. I've been a real failure as a spiritual leader in this home. I never meant for it to be this way. I guess the pressures of my job and providing *things* for my family got in the way of giving them what they need the most.
MOTHER:	I can't think of any better time than Christmas for us to re-dedicate our lives to the Lord.
FATHER:	I was just thinking the same thing. We're in for a family "first." Dad's gonna pray! Girls, where's your brother?
JOHNNY:	*(entering from stage right, sad)* Here I am. What did I do wrong this time?
FATHER:	I'm the one who's been wrong, son. Come over here. *(He hugs Johnny who is completely surprised and uncomfortable.)* Family, let's pray.

(The children don't know what to do. The Mother takes Father's and Wendy's hand, and Margaret, Sarah, and Johnny join the circle. Father is slow and uncertain as he prays.)

Dear God, we have been so far away from You. Please forgive me. I'm sort of rusty at this praying business, but I want to ask You to help us start putting You first in our family. We have a lot of catching up to do in teaching the children. Help us, Lord. *(Pause)* In Jesus' name, Amen.

| MOTHER: | This is wonderful! It makes me want to tell everyone about the Lord. Honey, isn't there something we could do? I know this is Christmas |

27

Eve, but surely we could come up with something. I could bake some cookies.

JOHNNY: What are you guys talking about?

SARAH: I know. We could make a manger scene in the front yard.

WENDY: *(catching her idea)*
            Sure, we could round up the neighbor kids we babysit. It's still early.

SARAH: Can we, Mom?

JOHNNY: Would somebody tell me what's going on?

FATHER: *(impatient)* Hush, Johnny . . . I mean. . . eh, come here, son. I'm gonna read you a story.

(They go to the couch and sit down beside each other. Father picks up the family Bible, blows the dust off, opens it to read.)

Sarah and Wendy go out the "front door" and out into the congregation where they invite children to play "nativity." They began to form the scene at stage left.

SARAH: Here, Jennifer, you'll make a perfect Mary. Brian, you be the angel.

BRIAN: I want to be a camel.

WENDY: Come on, Brian.

BRIAN: *(whining)* Oh, awright . . .

WENDY: Billy, you be Joseph.

As Sarah goes back into the house to bring out a box of old clothes, Wendy assembles the scene. Some of the children could have their own costumes

28

hidden in places around the sanctuary as they had gone back home to get them. Their mothers might help them dress, then send them "out to play." As the nativity unfolds, Father is reading to Johnny from the Bible.

FATHER: In the sixth month, God sent the angel Gabriel to Nazareth, a town in Galilee, to a virgin pledged to be married to a man named Joseph, a descendant of David. (Luke 1:26-27 NIV)

Choir: *"Cherish That Name"* by Lanny Wolfe or other appropriate song

WENDY: We need some shepherds. Jose, Susan, you be shepherds.

LITTLE CHILD: Can I be a lamb?

SARAH: Sure, you can be a lamb.

FATHER: *(reading)* And there were shepherds living in the fields nearby, keeping watch over their flocks by night. An angel of the Lord shone around them, and the glory of the Lord appeared to them, and they were terrified. *(Music begins.)* And the angel said to them, "Do not be afraid, I bring you good news of great joy that will be for all people. Today in the town of David, a Savior has been born to you. He is Christ the Lord. (Luke 2:8-12 NIV)

Choir: *"While Shepherds Watched Their Flocks by Night"*

SARAH: This is fun! Hey, now we need some wise men.

WENDY: I'll get them.

(She goes up the aisle and brings back three children, one being dragged by the hand.)

JIMMY: I was watching cartoons . . .

WENDY: Come on, Jimmy. This is *real* life. You'll have fun.

FATHER: After Jesus was born in Bethlehem, wise men from the East came to Jerusalem saying, "We saw His star in the East and we're coming to worship Him."

Choir: *"We Three Kings"* or other appropriate song

MOTHER: Oh, honey, just look at the children. Isn't that sweet?

FATHER: This is going to be our best Christmas in years. And it's all your "fault," Margaret.

MARGARET: Isn't the Lord good to us? I'll always remember this Christmas.

Lights dim and focus on the children's nativity scene.

Choir: *"O Holy Night"*

Pastor's Remarks and Invitation

Choir and audience: *"Thou Didst Leave Thy Throne"*
"Silent Night"

AN EPIPHANY PLAY

by Kathy Webb

Staging & Props: All Choir members wear crowns. Divide speaking parts as you wish. Props needed are a large star, a manger, and 3 gift boxes.

Junior Choir enters wearily from the side or back:

1. My feet hurt!

2. How much longer 'til we get there?

3. This gift box weights a ton.

4. Oh yeah? I'll trade you. I've got the *gold* box. It's **really** heavy.

5. "Call ahead and ask for directions," I said. "But, NO. We know where it is," you said. "We know that neighborhood. All we have to do is follow the star. Well, now where are we?

All: Lost, Lost, LOST!

Sing: *"From a Distant Home"* or *"We Three Kings"*

6. Wait! Look! (Point to the star) There's the star. We didn't lose our way!

All: We're here. We made it! Yea! Yea!

7. I guess you *were* right. The star *was* moving to the right spot.

8. All that travel paid off in the end!

Sing: *"The First Noel"* (verse 2)

9.   But who is Emmanuel? Look at all those people! Which one is God's chosen one? How can we find Emmanuel in this crowd?

10.   Hey, over here—this guy looks like he might know.

(All go over to Herod.)

Herod: Who are you?

11.   We are the wiseones. We are seeking the new ruler God has sent. Who are you?

Herod: I am Herod, all-knowing ruler of this land.

12.   Then you can tell us where to find Emmanuel!!

All: Tell us! Yes, tell us!!

Herod: Uh, um, just a minute . . . *(confers with associates)*. Well, well, we don't know either. But, *please* come and *tell* us when you find this new ruler so we can—uh . . . *welcome* Emmanuel, too. Good-bye. There you go. Thank you, thank you for coming.

13.   *(Walking away down the center aisle)* Hmmmm, I just don't trust that guy.

14.   Me either. What's he up to?

15.   Look, look—a beautiful woman. She reminds me of a perfect rose. She must be the one! Remember the prophecy, "Lo, How a Rose?"

All: Oh, right! Yes! *(etc.) (Run over to her.)*

Sing: *"Lo, How a Rose"* (verse 1)

Then all kneel down and say: Hail! Hail! Emmanuel!

16. She's a rose for sure. You are the **Promised One,** aren't you?

Woman: No.

All: *(disappointed)* Oh . . .

17. Look, look over here! I've found the Promised One— *(pick out a strong, big man or woman.)* I'm **sure** he (she) has to be strong to make all the valleys high and mountains low! Right?

All: Right! Right!

Sing: *"Toda Le Tierra"* (or *"Lift Up Your Heads, Ye Mighty Gates,"* (verse 1) *and/or do the following as cheerleaders:*

18. Lift up your heads,

All: O ye gates.

19. Lift them up,

All: O everlasting doors.

20. And the King of Glory

All: Shall come in.

21. Who is the King of Glory?

All: The Lord strong & mighty, might in battle.

22. *(Louder)* **Who is the King of Glory?**

All: The Lord strong & mighty, mighty in battle.

23. Lift up your heads,

All: O ye gates.

24. Lift them up,

All: O everlasting doors.

25. Al the King of Glory,

All: Shall—come—in—YEA!!

Then everyone bows and says: Hurrah for Emmanuel!

Man(woman):
> No, no I'm not the one you're seeking. Sorry. I don't know where to look either.

26. How about someone *old* and *wise*. Emmanuel is very wise and we all know old people have great wisdom. How about . . . *her (him)?*

All: OK! Yes! True! True!

Sing: *"O Come, O Come Emmanuel"* (verse 2)

All kneel down and say: Hail Emmanuel.

27. *Are you* Emmanuel?

Man (woman):
> No.

All: Ah . . . *(sit down)*

28. We're running out of ideas.

29. We're running out of energy.

30. We're running out of time.

All: Now what?

31. Look—this has **got** to be the one. *(Points to the pastor)* S/he's **right under the star.** S/he looks official. S/he's got a great outfit. S/he's in the front. In short, S/he looks like a leader. And Emmanuel is a **Leader,** a **Ruler. Right?**

All: Right! *(Start to kneel again.)*

32. Wait! Let's check this out first. **Are you Emmanuel?**

Pastor (shakes his/her head): Try the manger. (or over there.)

33.   What? Wait a minute! What are you saying? A little baby?

All: You're kidding! I don't believe it! It's joke! *(etc.)*

34.   Well, I guess there's no harm in asking . . . Are you the promised one, Baby!

35.   Wait, babies can't talk.

36.   But look, the baby is smiling at us.

37.   Hey, that's cute, that makes **me** smile.

38.   There's something special about that baby.

39.   Babies do grow up, too. Who knows what this baby will be when it's grown?

40.   The *star* tells us. This is a **special** child. *We found Emmanuel!*

41.   God is with us in this little baby.

42.   All of us were babies once, too. I think the star is over **all of us.** We are all part of God's plan.

43.   And we're all still growing, too!

44.   This star points to **all** of us. God is with each of us.

45.   This song is for us all, too.

Sing: *"On This Day, Earth Shall Ring"*

46.   Let us pray: Thank you God, for coming to be with us. Thank you for Emmanuel, who shows us the promise which is in each of us. Amen.

Then all kneel down with gifts, say softly: Hail, hail, Emmanuel.

Sing: *"What Child is This"* (with the congregation)

> *Choir exits or is seated during the last verse.*

CALM ON THE LISTENING EAR OF NIGHT

Calm on the listening ear of night
Come heaven's melodious strains,
Where wild Judea stretches far
Her silver-mantled plains.
Celestial choirs from courts above
Shed sacred glories there;
And angels, with their sparkling lyres,
Make music on the air.

The answering hills of Palestine
Send back the glad reply;
And greet, from all their holy heights,
The day-spring from on high.
O'er the blue depths of Galilee
There comes a holier calm,
And Sharon waves, in solemn praise,
Her silent groves of palm.

"Glory to God!" the sounding skies
Loud with their anthems ring,
"Peace to the earth good-will to all,
From heaven's eternal King!"
Light on thy hills, Jerusalem!
The Savior now is born:
More bright on Bethlehem's joyous plains
Breaks the first Christmas morn.

E. H. Sears

THE ANGEL'S MESSAGE

Angel messenger sent earthward,
Angel host attendant came;
Angel choir and angel carol
Angel message to proclaim.

"Fear ye not! Behold I bring you
These good tidings of great joy."
"Gloria in excelsis Deo,"
The angelic song employ.

"Unto you is born a Savior,
Unto us a Son is given;
Angels catch the angel message,
Angels voice that theme to Heaven."

Shepherds hear the angel message,
As they watch upon the plain,
With supernal light illumined,
And they heard the sweet refrain:

"Fear ye not! Behold I bring you
These good tidings of great joy."
"Gloria in excelsis Deo,"
The angelic song employ.

Angels and archangels hymning,
Lo the hills reverberate—
Angel message to us bringing,
God the Son is incarnate.

Warren Randolph Yeakel, 1896

HARK, HARK! MY SOUL!

Hark, Hark! my soul! angelic songs are swelling
O'er earth's green fields and ocean's wave-beat shore:
How sweet the truth those blessed strains are telling
Of that new life when sin shall be no more.

Far, far away, like bells at ev'ning pealing,
The voice of Jesus sounds o'er land and sea,
And laden souls by thousands meekly stealing,
Kind shepherd, turn their weary steps to Thee.

Onward we go, for still we hear them singing,
"Come, weary soul, for Jesus bids you come;
And thro' the dark, its echoes sweetly ringing,
The music of the Gospel leads us home.

Angels, sing on! your faithful watches keeping;
Sing us sweet fragments on the songs above,
Till morning's joy shall end the night of weeping,
And life's long shadows break in cloudless love.

F. W. Faber

DEAR LITTLE STRANGER

Low in a manger—dear little Stranger,
Jesus, the wonderful Savior, was born;
There was none to receive Him, none to believe Him,
None but the angels were watching that morn.

Angels descending, over Him bending,
Chanted a tender and silent refrain;
Then a wonderful story told of His glory,
Unto the shepherds on Bethlehem's plain.

Dear little Stranger, born in a manger,
Maker and Monarch, and Savior of all;
I will love Thee forever! Grieve Thee? No never!
Thou didst for me make Thy bed in a stall.

Charles H. Gabriel, 1900

CHRISTMAS

In another land and time,
Long ago and far away,
Was a little Baby born,
On the first glad Christmas day.

Words of truth and deeds of love,
Filled his life from day to day;
So that all the world was blest,
On the first glad Christmas day.

Little children did He love,
With a tender love alway;
So should little children be
Always glad on Christmas day.

Author Unknown

A GIFT FROM HEAVEN

Just a little Baby,
Jesus was His name,
Bringing joy and gladness
When from heaven He came.

Angels brought the message
Of the Baby's birth;
Said He was the Savior,
Sent to all the earth.

Ida F. Leyda, 1915

ON THE HILLS OF JUDAH

'Twas on the hills of Judah,
One bright and starry night,
That shepherds heard the singing,
And saw the heavenly light.

It was the angel chorus,
The song from heaven above.
Telling the glad, sweet story
Of God's great gift of love.

For God so loved all people,
He gave His only son,
To be a friend and helper,
And Savior to each one.

Ida F. Leyda, 1916

STORY OF THE WISE MEN

Long ago the glorious Christmas star,
Guided wise men from afar,
To the little town of Bethlehem,
To the Savior of us all.

Over hill, across desert sand,
Slowly toward the Holy land,
With them precious loving gifts they bring,
Asking for the newborn King.

When they saw the Child they all rejoiced,
Worshiped Him with tender voice,
Bowing low, presented gifts of love
To the Christ-Child from above.

Ida F. Leyda, 1916

ONE SOLITARY LIFE

Here is a man who was born in an obscure village, the child of a peasant woman. He grew up in still another obscure village.

He worked in a carpenter shop until he was thirty, then for three years he was an itinerant preacher.

He never wrote a book. He never held an office. He never had a family or owned a house. He didn't go to college. He never visited a big city. He never traveled two hundred miles from the place where he was born.

He did none of the things one usually associates with greatness. He had no credentials but himself.

While still a young man, the tide of public opinion turning against him. his friends ran away. One of them denied him.

He was turned over to his enemies and went through the mockery of a trial. He was nailed to a cross between two thieves. While he was dying, his executioners gambled for his clothing, the only property he had on earth.

When he was dead he was taken down and laid in a borrowed grave through the pity of a friend.

Nineteen wide centuries have come and gone, and today he is the centerpiece of the human race and the leader of the column of progress.

I am far within the mark when I say that all the armies that ever marched, and all the navies that ever were built, and all the parliaments that ever sat, and all the kings that ever reigned, put together, have not affected life on this earth as powerfully as has that one solitary life.

Author Unknown

A GLAD NEW YEAR

Ah, dearest Jesus, Holy child,
   Make Thee a bed, soft, undefiled
Within my heart, that it may be
   A quiet chamber, kept for Thee.

My heart for very joy does leap
   My lips no more can silence keep,
I too must sing with joyful tongue
   That sweetest ancient cradle song.

Glory to God in highest Heaven,
   Who unto man His Son has given,
While angels sing with pious mirth
   A glad New Year to all the earth!

Martin Luther

A CHRISTMAS CREED

I believe in Jesus Christ and in the beauty of the gospel that
      began in Bethlehem.

I believe in him who the kings of the earth ignored,
    and the proud can never understand,
    Whose path was among the common people,
    Whose welcome came from those of hungry hearts.

I believe in him who proclaimed the love of God to be
      invincible,
    Whose cradle was a mother's arms,
    Whose home in Nazareth had love for its only wealth,
    Who looked at men and made them see what His love saw in
      them,
    Who by his love brought sinners back to purity
    And lifted human weakness up to meet the strength of God.

I confess my everlasting need of God: the need of forgiveness
    for my greed and selfishness,
    The need of life for empty soul,
    The need of warmth for heart grown cold.

I acknowledge the glory of all that is like Christ:
    The steadfastness of friends
    The blessedness of home,
    The beauty of compassion,
    The courage of those who dare to resist all passion and hate.

I believe that only by love expressed shall the earth at length be
      purified,
    And I acknowledge in Christ
    A faith that sees beyond our present evil,
    And I pray that this redemption may begin in me now in this
      Christmas season as I pray.

Walter Russell Bowie

A CHRISTMAS PRAYER

Loving Father, help us remember the birth of Jesus, that we may share in the song of the angels, the gladness of the shepherds and the wisdom of the wise men.

Close the door of hate and open the door of love all the world over.
Let kindness come with every gift and good desires with every greeting.
Deliver us from evil by the blessing which Christ brings and teach us to be merry with clean hearts.

May the Christmas morning make us happy to be your children and the Christmas evening bring us to our beds with grateful thoughts, forgiving and forgiven, for Jesus' sake. Amen.

Robert Louis Stevenson (1850–1894)